Allah's name I begin with,
the utmost Kind, the ever Merciful.

Presented by
Ghousia Masjid Institute

ISIS:
State of Ignorance

A reflection on Islam and moderation,
extremism and terrorism, and the fitnah of ISIS (Daesh)

Muhammad Imdad Hussain Pirzada

AL-KARAM
PUBLICATIONS

ISBN 978-0-9569388-6-2

First Edition (2015)

Published by
Al-Karam Publications
Eaton Hall, Retford, Nottinghamshire, DN22 0PR, England, United Kingdom
www.alkarampublications.com

Edited, designed and typeset by Bakhtyar H Pirzada al-Azhari
info@alkarampublications.com

Printed by Mega Printing in Turkey

Abbreviations used in the book:
🌸 *salla'Llahu 'alayhi wa sallam*, Allah bless him and grant him peace.
[*as*]   *alayhi'l-salam*, upon him be peace.
[*ra*]   *radiya'Llahu anhu/anha*, Allah be pleased with him/her.

Contents

The *Fitnah* of ISIS   31-45

Foreword

All praise is for Allah, the utmost Kind, the ever Merciful. Peace and blessings be upon the beloved and sublime Messenger Muhammad ﷺ, the Mercy to all the worlds.

In an age of growing uncertainties and confusion, the need to highlight the true teachings of Islam in view of the intricate issues of the modern world cannot be underestimated. For this reason, it is very important that a clear and easily comprehensible message regarding Islam goes out to all corners of the globe, so that those who are yearning for the truth find a genuine message which is rooted in religious and scholarly authority and is free from any distortion and misinterpretation.

This concise book explains key themes and terminologies of concepts within Islam, whilst relating them to the world we live in. One of the greatest challenges faced by the followers of Islam today is the misrepresentation of Islam's principles, values, concepts and terms. Terrorists attempt to use Islam to justify their extreme intentions, distorting and misquoting religious concepts in order to brainwash others towards their way of thinking and to further their own concealed aims.

Organisations and groups with extremist tendencies leading to militancy and terrorism, in particular the so-called Islamic State of Iraq and Syria (ISIS), also referred to as ISIL and more appropriately as Daesh, are tarnishing the image of Islam through their distortion of concepts such as *jihad* (strive) and *khilafah* (caliphate). Members and supporters of ISIS are guilty of committing a great injustice, not merely against humanity but also against the religion of Islam, by referring to this religion of peace in order to justify their own brutal and criminal conduct of violence and terror, persecution of minorities and other religious groups, recruitment of child soldiers, sexual violence and slavery, beheadings and mass executions, as well as destruction of cultural and religious heritage, Muslim and otherwise.

This falsification of theological and legal discourses coupled with extreme and violent practice and behaviour is the cause of growing confusion, mistrust and unrest in various parts of our world. Not only for people from different communities, but also for the Muslim youth – particularly those uneducated in religion, some of whom are becoming lured into thinking that activities and ventures of these groups are part of some religious duty. They could not be any further away from the truth than this.

This book presents the discourse of Shaykh Muhammad Imdad Hussain Pirzada in relation to understanding moderation in Islam, and analysing extremism and terrorism in light of Islam. With reference to the recent phenomenon associated with ISIS or Daesh, increasingly being referred to as Daeshism, a brief study of the Qur'anic term *fitnah*, meaning strife and corruption, is also provided. Written in the author's own unique and straightforward style, this book is an important and worthy read.

Bakhtyar H Pirzada al-Azhari
July 2015

Chapter One

Islam and Moderation

Today Islam is being linked with extremism, fanaticism and terrorism. Therefore, it is important to express Islam using a word that actually reflects its essence and spirit as well as its governing principle. That single descriptive word is 'moderation' (*i'tidal*, *wasatiyyah*).

What is Islam? Islam is the name given to moderation in every deed, every creed, and every trait; in everything.

In the Arabic Language, the word *wast* refers to the central point that is right in the middle between two end points, i.e. the balance between two extremes. A person who remains steadfast committing himself to the balance at the middle does not fall victim to extremism. For this reason, *wast* is described as being the 'best' and being of 'moderation' because it remains pure and free from going towards either of the extremes, i.e. *ifrat* (excess, too much) and *tafrit* (negligence, too little).

Islam is a religion of moderation because it is free from both *ifrat* and *tafrit*, i.e. excess and negligence. For Allah's Messenger, the Prophet Muhammad 鄛, said: "From among the deeds, the best deed is moderation. The religion of Allah (Most High) is in the middle between excess and negligence; and a good deed is in the middle between two bad deeds."[1] In this prophetic tradition (*hadith*), the two bad deeds refer to excess and negligence; and a good deed, i.e. moderation, is in the middle between these two. Just as extravagance and miserliness are both bad habits, and in the middle between these two lies generosity, which symbolises moderation and is a good habit.

Abu Darda' [*ra*] reports that the Prophet Muhammad ﷺ said: "The people who adopt moderation, their accountability (in the hereafter) will be made easy."[2]

Furthermore, 'Abdullah ibn 'Abbas [*ra*] reports that the Prophet Muhammad ﷺ said: "Indeed good guidance, good mannerism and moderation are one segment from the twenty-five segments of prophethood."[3]

Moderation is the way of the Muslim community

Allah (Most High) says:

وَكَذَٰلِكَ جَعَلْنَٰكُمْ أُمَّةً وَسَطًا

*"And in this way, We have made you (O Muslims!)
the community of moderation."* [Qur'an 2:143]

Jabir ibn 'Abdillah [*ra*] reports that the Prophet Muhammad ﷺ three times repeated the statement: "O people! Be moderate. For

---

[1] Al-Suyuti, *al-Jami' al-Saghir*, p. 352, hadith 5708; al-Bayhaqi, *Shu'ab al-Iman*, vol. 3, p. 402, hadith 3887.
[2] Ahmad, *Musnad Ahmad ibn Hanbal*, vol. 5, p. 198.
[3] Abu Dawud, *Sunan Abi Dawud*, book of *al-adab*, chapter 2, hadith 4776.

indeed Allah (Most High) does not tire out (from giving reward) until you tire out (from performing deeds)."[1]

Moderation in worship

Allah (Most High) says:

وَلَا تَجْهَرْ بِصَلَاتِكَ وَلَا تُخَافِتْ بِهَا وَٱبْتَغِ بَيْنَ ذَٰلِكَ سَبِيلًا ۝

"And do not be too loud (reciting the Qur'an) in your (congregational) prayer, and do not be too quiet in it, rather seek a (moderate) way between these two." [Qur'an 17:110]

Consider the following prophetic traditions:

1. Jabir ibn Samurah [*ra*] relates that he used to perform the prayer with the Prophet Muhammad ﷺ; the Prophet's prayer and his sermon were moderate.[2]

2. Sayyidah 'A'ishah [*ra*] reports that the Prophet Muhammad ﷺ said: "O people! Do what you can; for Allah (Most High) does not tire out (from giving reward) until you tire out (from performing deeds). The most beloved deed to Allah (Most High) is the one which is done regularly, even if it is little."[3]

3. Anas [*ra*] relates that three individuals visited the quarters of the beloved wives of the Prophet Muhammad ﷺ and asked them regarding the manner of the Prophet's worship. When they were informed about his manner of worship, they considered it to be less and said: "What is our value

---

[1] Ibn Majah, *Sunan Ibn Majah*, chapters of *al-zuhd*, chapter 28, hadith 4241.
[2] Muslim, *Sahih Muslim*, book of *al-jumu'ah*, chapter 13, hadith 2004.
[3] Al-Bukhari, *Sahih al-Bukhari*, book of *al-libas*, chapter 43, hadith 5861.

compared to the Prophet ﷺ? His past and future deeds that are contrary-to-the-preferred (*khilaf al-awla*) have all been pardoned." One of them then said: "In any case, I will always spend the whole night in worship." The second one said: "I will always maintain fasting and will never miss a fast." The third one said: "I will stay away from women and will never get married."

Later Allah's Messenger ﷺ came to them and said: "You people have said such-and-such a thing. Listen! By Allah! I am the most fearful of Allah (Most High) from amongst you, yet I keep the fasts and I also leave the fasts, I offer the prayer (at night) and I also sleep at night, and I also get married to women. Thus whoever turns away from my practice, he is not upon my path."[1]

4.　Sa'd ibn Abi Waqas [*ra*] reports that the matter concerning 'Uthman ibn Maz'un [*ra*] became well known that he had decided to stay away from women and not get married. The Prophet Muhammad ﷺ called for him and said to him: "O 'Uthman! I have not been ordered to pursue monasticism! Have you turned away from my practice?" He replied: "No, O Messenger of Allah!" The Prophet Muhammad ﷺ then stated: "It is my practice that I offer the prayer at night and I also sleep, I keep the fasts and I also leave the fasts, and I also get married to women. Thus whoever turns away from my practice, he is not from amongst us. O 'Uthman! Verily your family has a right over you, and your self has a right over you too."[2]

Islam does not permit the complete abandoning of the world, nor does it tolerate the abandoning of worship to indulge

---

[1] Al-Bukhari, *Sahih al-Bukhari*, book of *al-nikah*, chapter 1, hadith 5063.
[2] Al-Darimi, *Sunan al-Darimi*, book of *al-nikah*, chapter 3.

only in worldly pleasures and joys. Islam teaches balance and moderation between the world and worship, for both are essential for a person's success in life.

5.   Sayyidah 'A'ishah [*ra*] reports that the Prophet Muhammad ﷺ said: "Whenever any one of you feels sleepy during prayer, he should go to sleep until his drowsiness comes to an end. For if any one of you performs the prayer whilst in the state of being drowsy, he will not be aware (of what he is saying), possibly seeking forgiveness (in his mind) and (in reality) swearing at himself."[1]

6.   Abu Hurayrah [*ra*] reports that the Prophet Muhammad ﷺ said: "When one of you leads others in prayer, he should lighten the prayer. For there are the weak, the sick and the elderly (among the worshippers). And when one of you performs the prayer on his own, he can lengthen his prayer as much as he likes."[2]

When the Prophet Muhammad ﷺ would perform the prayer on his own, he would prolong it to the extent that his feet would be swollen. But when he would lead others in prayer, then he would shorten the prayer according to his followers.

7.   Abu Mas'ud [*ra*] relates that a person said: "O Messenger of Allah! I perform the dawn prayer (*fajr*) a little late because so-and-so recites a very lengthy recitation in the dawn prayer." The Prophet Muhammad ﷺ became so angry that Abu Mas'ud [*ra*] had not seen him become this angry before. Then the Prophet Muhammad ﷺ stated: "O people! Some from amongst you are inducing people's dislike towards religion. So the person who leads others in prayer, he should

---

[1] Al-Bukhari, *Sahih al-Bukhari*, book of *al-wudu'*, chapter 53, hadith 212.
[2] ibid., book of *al-adhan*, chapter 62, hadith 703.

shorten the prayer, for behind him there are the weak, the elderly and those with duties to go to."[1]

8.   Jabir ibn 'Abdillah [*ra*] relates that Mu'adh ibn Jabal [*ra*] led the nightfall prayer (*'isha*) and recited *Surat al-Baqarah* in it (Chapter 2 of the Qur'an). When a complaint regarding this lengthy prayer was made to the Prophet Muhammad ﷺ, he repeated the following statement three times: "O Mu'adh! Are you placing people in *fitnah* (i.e. causing strife)?"[2]

Moderation in preaching and giving counsel

Abu Wa'il relates that 'Abdullah ibn Mas'ud [*ra*] would preach and given counsel to the people every Thursday. A person once said to him: "O 'Abdullah! It is my desire that you counsel us everyday." 'Abdullah [*ra*] replied: "What stops me from doing so is that I do not want to tire you out, thus I take into consideration your circumstances. Just as the Prophet Muhammad ﷺ, being concerned about our exhaustion, would take into consideration our situations when preaching and counselling us."[3]

Moderation in social conduct

1.   Abu Hurayrah [*ra*] reports that the Prophet Muhammad ﷺ said: "Moderation is the best code of conduct."[4] [*khayr al-umur awsatuha*]

2.   The Prophet Muhammad ﷺ stated: "The individual who possesses three certain qualities will achieve excellence and greatness like what was granted to the children of Prophet

---

[1] Al-Bukhari, *Sahih al-Bukhari*, book of *al-adhan*, chapter 63, hadith 704.
[2] ibid., book of *al-adab*, chapter 74, hadith 6106.
[3] ibid., book of *al-'ilm*, chapter 13, hadith 70.
[4] Ibn al-Athir al-Jazari, *Jami' al-Usul*, vol. 1, p. 317, chapter 2 (*al-iqtisad*).

Dawud (David [as])." The Companions asked: "What are those three qualities?" The Prophet Muhammad ﷺ replied: "Being just in happiness and in anger, being moderate in prosperity and in poverty, and being fearful of Allah (Most High) in private and in public."[1]

Moderation in consumption

Allah (Most High) says:

$$وَكُلُواْ وَٱشْرَبُواْ وَلَا تُسْرِفُوٓاْ إِنَّهُۥ لَا يُحِبُّ ٱلْمُسْرِفِينَ ۝$$

"And eat and drink, and do not exceed the limits. Verily Allah does not like the exceeders of limits." [*Qur'an* 7:31]

In the commentary of this verse, al-Alusi writes that a Christian doctor once said to 'Ali ibn al-Husayn ibn Waqid: "There is nothing concerning the knowledge of medicine in your Qur'an." 'Ali ibn al-Husayn replied: "Allah (Most High) has expressed all of medicine in just half of a verse, i.e. *'And eat and drink, and do not exceed the limits'.*" The doctor responded: "But what has your Messenger said concerning medicine?" 'Ali ibn al-Husayn replied: "Our Messenger ﷺ has gathered medicine into a few words, i.e. 'the stomach is home to all illnesses, and its protection is the basis of all cures, and only give to each limb of the body what it deserves'." Upon hearing this, the Christian doctor commented: "Your Qur'an and your Messenger have not left anything of medicine for Galen!"[2] In other words, in just these two sentences the basics of the principles of medicine have been comprehensively gathered in such a manner that the medicine of Claudius Galen

---

[1] Al-Qurtubi, *Al-Jami' li Ahkam al-Qur'an*, in the commentary of 34:13.
[2] Al-Alusi, *Ruh al-Ma'ani fi Tafsir al-Qur'an al-'Azim wa'l-Sab' al-Mathani*, in the commentary of 7:31.

9

has been encompassed within them. In short, if an individual does not exceed the limits in his eating and drinking, rather adopts moderation, then his stomach remains healthy and the individual remains protected from illness.

Moderation in expenditure

Allah (Most High) says:

وَٱلَّذِينَ إِذَآ أَنفَقُواْ لَمْ يُسْرِفُواْ وَلَمْ يَقْتُرُواْ وَكَانَ بَيْنَ ذَٰلِكَ قَوَامًا ۝

"And those (pious ones) when they spend, they are neither extravagant nor miserly, rather their manner between them is of moderation."
[*Qur'an* 25:67]

When 'Abd al-Malik ibn Marwan enquired about spending at the time of marriage of his daughter with 'Umar ibn 'Abd al-Aziz [*ra*], 'Umar ibn 'Abd al-Aziz [*ra*] stated: "A good deed is in between two bad deeds." This meant that moderation in spending is a good deed, and that lies in between *israf* (extravagance) and *iqtar* (miserliness), both of which are bad deeds.[1]

Moderation in charity

Providing assistance to the poor and needy carries great merit and excellence in Islam. In this regard, the statement of the Prophet Muhammad ﷺ is very clear: "He is not a (complete) believer who eats satiated himself whilst his neighbour remains hungry."[2]

---

[1] Sadr al-Afadil Maulana Na'im al-Din Muradabadi, *Tafsir Khaza'in al-'Irfan*, in the commentary of 25:67.
[2] Al-Tabrizi, *Mishkat al-Masabih*, book of *al-adab*, chapter of *al-shafaqah wa'l-rahmah 'ala'l-khalq* (15), section 3, hadith 4991.

However, moderation is also needed in giving charity, just as Allah (Most High) says:

$$
\text{وَلَا تَجْعَلْ يَدَكَ مَغْلُولَةً إِلَىٰ عُنُقِكَ وَلَا تَبْسُطْهَا كُلَّ ٱلْبَسْطِ فَتَقْعُدَ مَلُومًا مَّحْسُورًا ﴿٢٩﴾}
$$

"And do not keep your hand bound to your neck, and do not extend it either to its full extent, lest you end up sitting blamed and destitute."
[*Qur'an* 17:29]

In other words, do not become so miserly that you end up not helping those in need and the people begin to blame you, and do not become so extravagant that your own wealth comes to an end and you are forced to beg yourself. Rather, maintain moderation and balance in both circumstances of prosperity and poverty.

Moderation in friendship and in enmity

Allah (Most High) says:

$$
\text{وَلَا يَجْرِمَنَّكُمْ شَنَـانُ قَوْمٍ عَلَىٰ أَلَّا تَعْدِلُوا۟ ٱعْدِلُوا۟ هُوَ أَقْرَبُ لِلتَّقْوَىٰ}
$$

"And do not let hatred for a people incite you towards not being just. Be just, that is closer to God-fearingness." [*Qur'an* 5:8]

Consider the following two prophetic traditions:

1.   Abu Hurayrah [*ra*] reports that the Prophet Muhammad ﷺ said: "Maintain gentle affection towards your friend, for it is possible that one day he may become your foe. And maintain gentle enmity towards your foe, for it is possible

11

that one day he may become your friend."[1]

2. Whilst admonishing his son, Luqman the Wise [*ra*] said to him: "O my beloved son! Do not be so sweet that you end up being swallowed; and do not be so sour that you end up being spat out."[2]

Moderation in the battlefield

Allah (Most High) says:

$$\text{وَقَٰتِلُواْ فِى سَبِيلِ ٱللَّهِ ٱلَّذِينَ يُقَٰتِلُونَكُمْ وَلَا تَعْتَدُوٓاْ} \\ \text{إِنَّ ٱللَّهَ لَا يُحِبُّ ٱلْمُعْتَدِينَ} \; ﴿١٩٠﴾$$

> *"And fight in the way of Allah those who fight you, and do not transgress. For indeed Allah does not like the transgressors."*
> [*Qur'an* 2:190]

Allah (Most High) also says:

$$\text{فَمَنِ ٱعْتَدَىٰ عَلَيْكُمْ فَٱعْتَدُواْ عَلَيْهِ بِمِثْلِ مَا ٱعْتَدَىٰ عَلَيْكُمْ} \\ \text{وَٱتَّقُواْ ٱللَّهَ وَٱعْلَمُوٓاْ أَنَّ ٱللَّهَ مَعَ ٱلْمُتَّقِينَ} \; ﴿١٩٤﴾$$

> *"So if anyone transgresses against you, then you may transgress against him in the same measure as he transgressed against you. And be fearful of Allah, and know that Allah is with the God-fearing."* [*Qur'an* 2:194]

Allah (Most High) further says:

---

[1] Al-Tirmidhi, *Sunan al-Tirmidhi*, chapters of *al-birr*, chapter 60, hadith 1997.
[2] Al-Suyuti, *Tafsir al-Durr al-Manthur fi'l-Tafsir al-Ma'thur*, in the commentary of 31:13.

$$وَجَزَٰٓؤُاْ سَيِّئَةٍ سَيِّئَةٌ مِّثْلُهَاۖ فَمَنْ عَفَا وَأَصْلَحَ فَأَجْرُهُۥ عَلَى ٱللَّهِۚ إِنَّهُۥ لَا يُحِبُّ ٱلظَّٰلِمِينَ ۝$$

"And the recompense for an evil is evil equal to it. But whoever forgives and sets things right, his reward is upon the generosity of Allah. Indeed He does not like the wrongdoers." [Qur'an 42:40]

In the first two verses, Allah (Most High) has granted permission to the Muslims that they may fight in defence against those who fight them; however, the condition is that they can only fight against those who are actually fighting them or preparing to do so. Those who are not directly involved in the battle, they cannot transgress against them, such as the women, the sick, the children, the elderly, the religious leaders, even animals and fruitful trees cannot be unnecessarily harmed.

In the first two verses, the requirements of justice and fairness have been fulfilled; in other words, the level of monetary loss or physical harm that you have received, you can only avenge for that (through law), but avenging for more than your loss suffered is itself a transgression, and Allah (Most High) does not like those who transgress. In the third verse, Allah (Most High) has encouraged forgiveness and pardon that if the one who has been wronged controls his emotions and forgives, then the benefit of this course of action would be that their enmity will turn into friendship in this world, and in the hereafter Allah (Most High) will grant him a great reward.

Readers! Ponder over the previous three verses once again: Islam is the first religion in this world which instructs justice and moderation with the enemy even at the time of the exchange of might and strength so that no innocent and non-criminal individual is murdered, and at the same time encourages forgiveness and pardon so that an atmosphere of peace and security can be created for all time. In this regard, consider the character of our beloved Prophet Muhammad 🕮:

1. Sayyidah 'A'ishah [*ra*] reports that Allah's Messenger 🕮 never took revenge for his own self from anyone.[1] The Prophet Muhammad 🕮 did not return evil for evil; rather, he forgave and pardoned.[2]

2. The non-Muslims of Makkah labelled the Prophet Muhammad 🕮 as a magician and a madman, caused him to suffer a social boycott, conspired to martyr him, forced him to migrate from Makkah, and upon martyring his paternal uncle Hamzah [*ra*], cut out his liver and chewed it; however, when the Prophet Muhammad 🕮 after eight years conquered Makkah, standing in the courtyard of the Ka'bah, he addressed those severe enemies with these noble words: "O people of Quraysh! What do you think as to how I will deal with you today?" They replied: "You are a noble Prophet, a noble brother, and the son of a noble brother; we are hopeful of good from you." The Prophet Muhammad 🕮 then stated: "Today I say the same thing to you which my brother Yusuf (Joseph [*as*]) said to his brothers. There is no hold from me on you today. Go! From me you are free."[3]

No example comparable to the exemplary display of the best of character and forgiveness demonstrated by the Prophet Muhammad 🕮 can be found in the history of humankind. Seeing this grandeur of the holy Prophet's nobility and

---

[1] Al-Bukhari, *Sahih al-Bukhari*, book of *al-adab*, chapter 80, hadith 6126.
[2] Al-Tirmidhi, *Sunan al-Tirmidhi*, book of *al-birr wa'l-silah*, chapter 69, hadith 2016.
[3] Pir Muhammad Karam Shah al-Azhari, *Sirat Diya' al-Nabi*, vol. 4, p. 445; Ibn Hajar al-'Asqalani, *Fath al-Bari*, vol. 8, p. 18.

generosity, the people of Makkah began to come forward in large numbers and they began to accept Islam at the blessed hands of the Prophet Muhammad ﷺ.

Islam is a religion of peace and security

Islam comes from the root word *salam* which means peace and security. When Muslims greet one another, they pray for peace and security for one another. Moreover, everyday Muslims raise their hands to Allah (Most High) and supplicate in the words: "O Allah! You are peace; from You is peace; and to You peace returns. O our Lord! Keep us alive in peace and enter us into the house of peace." The person who prays for peace and security for others on a daily basis and supplicates for peace and security for himself, who can be more peace-loving than him?

Islam has emphasised the promotion and spreading of peace. The Prophet Muhammad ﷺ clearly stated: "You will not enter Paradise until you believe, and you will not become believers until you love one another. Shall I not tell you about something if you act upon it, you will love one another? Spread peace amongst you!"[1]

Consider the following prophetic traditions:

1.   Fudalah ibn 'Ubayd [*ra*] relates that the Prophet Muhammad ﷺ stated on the occasion of the farewell pilgrimage: "Listen carefully! I inform you that a (complete) *mu'min* (believer) is that individual with whom all people (Muslim and non-Muslim) consider their lives and their properties to be safe; and a (complete) *Muslim* is that individual from whose tongue and hands all people (Muslim and non-Muslim) are safe; and a (complete) *mujahid* (one

---

[1] Muslim, *Sahih Muslim*, book of *al-iman*, chapter 21, hadith 194.

who strives) is that individual who struggles against his own self in the obedience of Allah (Most High); and a (complete) *muhajir* (one who migrates) is that individual who migrates from mistakes and sins."[1]

2.   'Abdullah ibn 'Amr ibn al-'As [*ra*] reports that a person once asked: "O Messenger of Allah! Which Islam is best?" The Prophet Muhammad ﷺ replied: "(The Islam of that individual is best) From whose tongue and hands all people (Muslim and non-Muslim) are safe."[2]

It becomes clear from this prophetic tradition (*hadith*) that the greatest Muslim is the one from whose tongue and whose hands all (Muslim and non-Muslim) people are safe. If any Muslim observes the prayers (*salat*), the fasting (*sawm*), the pilgrimage (*hajj*) and the prescribed alms (*zakat*), etc., but from his tongue and his hands the lives, dignity and properties of people are not safe, then he is not a good Muslim and will not be able to escape the punishment from Allah (Most High). Just as Abu Hurayrah [*ra*] narrates that the Prophet Muhammad ﷺ was asked: "So-and-so woman performs the prayer at night, fasts during the day, but harasses her neighbours with her ill-speech?" The Prophet Muhammad ﷺ replied: "There is no good in her; she will go to Hell."[3]

3.   Bara' ibn 'Azib [*ra*] relates that the Prophet Muhammad ﷺ said: "According to Allah (Most High), for the whole world to become ruined and destroyed is a lesser (incident) than the unlawful killing of any single (Muslim or non-Muslim)

---

[1] Ahmad, *Musnad Ahmad ibn Hanbal*, vol. 6, p. 21.
[2] ibid., vol. 2, p. 187.
[3] Hakim, *al-Mustadrak 'ala'l-Sahihayn*, vol. 4, p. 184, hadith 7304; Ahmad, *Musnad Ahmad ibn Hanbal*, vol. 2, p. 440.

individual."[1] This means that the whole world coming to an end is not such a great loss compared to the unlawful killing of any single person.

4. Hisham ibn Hakim [*ra*] reports that the Prophet Muhammad ﷺ said: "Allah (Most High) will punish those people who cause suffering to other people (Muslims and non-Muslims) in this world."[2]

Islam condemns *zulm* (oppression)

Observe the following verses in which Allah (Most High) says:

$$\text{وَٱللَّهُ لَا يُحِبُّ ٱلظَّٰلِمِينَ ۝}$$

"And Allah does not like the wrongdoers (zalimun)."
[*Qur'an* 3:57]

$$\text{أَلَا لَعْنَةُ ٱللَّهِ عَلَى ٱلظَّٰلِمِينَ ۝}$$

"Listen carefully! The curse of Allah is upon the wrongdoers (zalimun)."
[*Qur'an* 11:18]

$$\text{إِنَّ ٱلظَّٰلِمِينَ لَهُمْ عَذَابٌ أَلِيمٌ ۝}$$

"Indeed for the wrongdoers (zalimun) there is a painful torment."
[*Qur'an* 14:22]

$$\text{تِلْكَ حُدُودُ ٱللَّهِ فَلَا تَعْتَدُوهَا وَمَن يَتَعَدَّ حُدُودَ ٱللَّهِ}$$

---

[1] Al-Bayhaqi, *Shu'ab al-Iman*, vol. 4, p. 345, hadith 5344.
[2] Muslim, *Sahih Muslim*, book of *al-birr*, chapter 33, hadith 6657.

فَأُوْلَٰٓئِكَ هُمُ ٱلظَّٰلِمُونَ ۝

"These are the limits of Allah, so do not transgress them. And those who transgress the limits of Allah, they are the ones who are wrongdoers (zalimun)." [Qur'an 2:229]

وَلَا تَرْكَنُوٓاْ إِلَى ٱلَّذِينَ ظَلَمُواْ فَتَمَسَّكُمُ ٱلنَّارُ

"And do not incline towards those who have done wrong (zulm), lest the Fire touches you as well." [Qur'an 11:113]

In this particular verse, the people of Islam are being cautioned that they must not have any attachment or inclination towards the wrongdoing and oppressive people (*zalimun*), and they must remain distant from their respect, company and friendship. Otherwise, the fire of Hell in which these wrongdoers will burn, they may become deserving of that same fire too.

Consider the following prophetic traditions:

1. Abu Dharr [*ra*] reports from the Prophet Muhammad 🕌 who stated that Allah (Most High) says: "O my servants! I have forbidden *zulm* upon Myself, and I have forbidden it between you too, so do not commit *zulm* upon one another."[1]

2. Jabir ibn 'Abdillah [*ra*] relates that the Prophet Muhammad 🕌 said: "Beware of *zulm*, for *zulm* is the darkness of the Day of Judgement."[2]

3. Huzayfah [*ra*] reports that the Prophet Muhammad 🕌

---

[1] Muslim, *Sahih Muslim*, book of *al-birr*, chapter 15, hadith 6572.
[2] ibid., hadith 6576.

stated: "The wrongdoers (*zalimun*) and their helpers will go to Hell."[1]

4.   Ibn 'Umar [*ra*] relates that the Prophet Muhammad ﷺ said: "A Muslim is a brother to a Muslim. Neither should he commit *zulm* towards him, nor give him to the enemy."[2]

5.   Jabir [*ra*] reports that the Prophet Muhammad ﷺ said: "A person should help his brother, whether he is an oppressor (*zalim*) or the oppressed (*mazlum*). If his brother is an oppressor, he should stop him from this *zulm*; this is his help. And if his brother is the oppressed, he should help him."[3]

Islam is a religion of ease

Islam is a religion of ease; severity in its teachings should not be adopted, otherwise these teachings will become a burden. For Allah (Most High) says:

$$\text{يُرِيدُ ٱللَّهُ بِكُمُ ٱلْيُسْرَ وَلَا يُرِيدُ بِكُمُ ٱلْعُسْرَ}$$

"Allah intends ease for you, and does not intend hardship for you."
[*Qur'an* 2:185]

$$\text{لَا يُكَلِّفُ ٱللَّهُ نَفْسًا إِلَّا وُسْعَهَا}$$

"Allah does not make a person responsible for more than he can bear."
[*Qur'an* 2:286]

In this regard, consider the following prophetic traditions:

---

[1] Al-Suyuti, *al-Jami' al-Saghir*, vol. 2, p. 331, hadith 5356.
[2] Muslim, *Sahih Muslim*, book of *al-birr*, chapter 15, hadith 6578.
[3] ibid., chapter 16, hadith 6582.

1.   Sayyidah 'A'ishah [*ra*] reports that when the Prophet Muhammad ﷺ would be offered a choice between two things, he would select the easier one of the two so long as it was not a sin; and if it was a sin, he would be the most furthest away from it. Allah's Messenger ﷺ never took revenge for his own self from anyone.[1]

2.   Anas [*ra*] relates that the Prophet Muhammad ﷺ said: "Make things easy, and do not make things difficult. Give glad tidings, and do not cause dislike (of religion)."[2]

3.   Abu Hurayrah [*ra*] reports that a Bedouin once stood up and urinated inside the mosque, and the people then took hold of him. The Prophet Muhammad ﷺ said to the people: "Leave him alone and spill a bucket of water over his urine. For you have been sent to make things easy; you have not been sent to make things difficult."[3]

4.   Sayyidah 'A'ishah [*ra*] relates that the Prophet Muhammad ﷺ said: "O 'A'ishah! Indeed Allah is Compassionate, and He loves gentleness. What He gives upon gentleness, He does not give upon harshness."[4]

5.   Sayyidah 'A'ishah [*ra*] reports that the Prophet Muhammad ﷺ said: "Kindness is not to be found in anything except that it makes it beautiful, and kindness is not removed from anything except that it makes it defective."[5]

---

[1] Al-Bukhari, *Sahih al-Bukhari*, book of *al-adab*, chapter 80, hadith 6126.
[2] ibid., book of *al-'ilm*, chapter 12, hadith 69.
[3] ibid., book of *al-wudu'*, chapter 61, hadith 220.
[4] Muslim, *Sahih Muslim*, book of *al-birr*, chapter 23, hadith 6601.
[5] ibid., hadith 6602.

Chapter Two

Extremism and Terrorism

Two terms are generally used to describe incidents of severity and violence: One is 'extremism' and the other is 'terrorism'. Although both of these concepts are closely related, but there is a subtle difference between the too, which is as follows:

When an individual or a group moves away from the central and moderate position of its society, and an excess beyond the limit or a shortage well below the limit in ideology and viewpoint takes root, then this attitude of moving towards the extremes – *ifrat* (excess, too much) and *tafrit* (negligence, too little) – is called 'extremism'. And when severity and intensity takes further root in this extremism, then terrorism is born out of it. This means that terrorism is one form of extremism. In other words, every terrorist is an extremist because he takes the extreme practical step. It is not necessary, however, that every extremist is a terrorist because it is possible that his extremism has not yet reached such severity that he ends up pursuing the path of terrorism.

Islam and extremism

Extremism has been condemned strongly in Islamic teachings.

Consider some traditions in relation to this:

1. Ibn 'Abbas [*ra*] reports that the Prophet Muhammad ﷺ stated: "O people! Beware of crossing the limits in religion (extremism), for excessiveness in religion wiped out many people before you."[1]

2. 'Abdullah ibn Mas'ud [*ra*] relates that the Prophet Muhammad ﷺ repeated the following statement three times: "Zealots (extremists) will perish."[2] Imam al-Nawawi writes that zealots (*mutanatti'un*) mentioned in this prophetic tradition (*hadith*) refer to those people who cross the limits in their statements and actions.[3]

3. Abu Qalabah narrates that 'Abdullah ibn Mas'ud [*ra*] said: "Seek knowledge before the people of knowledge are no more. Listen carefully! Beware of extremism."[4] In other words, be quick in seeking knowledge; for it may be the case that scholars of moderation pass away and then extremist scholars mislead you.

It is clearly understood from these narrations that the end result and consequence of extremism is destruction and annihilation. Therefore, it has nothing to do with Islam, for Islam is a religion of peace and security, and moderation.

Islam and terrorism

With the aim of achieving political or religious objectives, to instil fear among people by the use of violence, murder and destruction

---

[1] Ibn Majah, *Sunan Ibn Majah*, chapters of *al-manasik*, chapter 63, hadith 3029.
[2] Muslim, *Sahih Muslim*, book of *al-'ilm*, chapter 4, hadith 6784.
[3] Al-Nawawi, *Sharh Sahih Muslim*, vol. 8, p. 266.
[4] Al-Darimi, *Sunan al-Darimi*, the *muqaddimah*, chapter 19.

is referred to as 'terrorism'. Numerous factors can contribute to the causes behind terrorism, such as poverty and deprivation, despair and lack of freedom, pain and suffering, usurping of rights and injustice, political or religious extremism, and so on. When such causative factors go beyond the limits, they may then adopt the form of terrorism.

In any case, Islam has absolutely no room for terrorism and the spreading of corruption and mischief. Islam strongly condemns violence, terror and brigandage (*hirabah*). It is the duty of Muslim rulers to use force in order to completely eradicate terrorism, just as Allah (Most High) says:

$$وَقَٰتِلُوهُمْ حَتَّىٰ لَا تَكُونَ فِتْنَةٌ$$

"And keep striving in jihad against them until mischief is no more."
[*Qur'an* 2:193]

One of the most distressing things about terrorism is that those committing acts of terrorism consider themselves to be right and others to be wrong, and then with the intention of correcting them, they consider their murder to be permissible.

Just as a sick person tastes a sweet thing to be bitter, and a bitter thing to be sweet; similarly, the terrorists consider their violence and corruption as being reform, whereas in reality they are themselves profoundly wrong. Just as Allah (Most High) says:

$$وَإِذَا قِيلَ لَهُمْ لَا تُفْسِدُوا فِي ٱلْأَرْضِ قَالُوٓا۟ إِنَّمَا نَحْنُ مُصْلِحُونَ ۝ أَلَآ إِنَّهُمْ هُمُ ٱلْمُفْسِدُونَ وَلَٰكِن لَّا يَشْعُرُونَ ۝$$

"And when it is said to them: "Do not spread corruption in the earth.""

They say: "We are only reformers." Beware! Indeed they themselves are the corrupters, but they do not realise." [*Qur'an* 2:11-12]

As an example, constructing a mosque is indeed a very virtuous deed, but constructing a mosque by looting someone's home is not permissible. In the same way, reforming bad people is a good deed, but spreading terrorism and perpetrating murder and mayhem is strongly not permissible.

Those among the Muslims who choose the path of extremism and terrorism, they too consider themselves to be good and proper Muslims, and they consider others to be wrong and out of the folds of Islam. Yet declaring someone as a non-Muslim is a matter that requires great care and caution.

For Ibn 'Umar [*ra*] reports that the Prophet Muhammad ﷺ said: "He who declares his Islamic brother to be an unbeliever (non-Muslim), then unbelief (*kufr*) will most certainly return to one of them two. If that person is indeed a non-Muslim then so he is, otherwise the one accusing the other of unbelief will become an unbeliever."[1] It is for this reason that Mufti Ahmad Yar Khan Na'imi writes that the scholars have stated: "If in the speech of a Muslim there are 99 meanings of unbelief and only one meaning of faith (*iman*), then he should not be labelled an unbeliever based upon this."[2]

Islam and suicide bombings

Suicide bombings are a form of terrorism, i.e. with the aim of achieving political or religious objectives, to blow oneself up with explosives in such a manner that causes others to be killed and become injured too. A suicide bomber is a double criminal,

---

[1] Muslim, *Sahih Muslim*, book of *al-iman*, chapter 26, hadith 216.
[2] Mufti Ahmad Yar Khan Na'imi, *Tafsir Nur al-'Irfan*, in the commentary of 49:12.

because on the one hand he kills himself, and on the other hand he kills others too. Whereas both of these assaults are strictly unlawful and forbidden.

Killing oneself (suicide)

Allah (Most High) says:

$$\text{وَلَا تَقۡتُلُوٓاْ أَنفُسَكُمۡ إِنَّ ٱللَّهَ كَانَ بِكُمۡ رَحِيمٗا}\ \text{(29)}$$

"And do not kill yourselves. Verily Allah is merciful towards you."
[Qur'an 4:29]

Abu Hurayrah [*ra*] reports that the Prophet Muhammad ﷺ stated: "The person who kills himself by leaping from a mountain (i.e. commits suicide), he will go to Hell and will forever be falling in Hell. And the person who commits suicide by consuming poison, he will have poison in his hands and will forever consume that poison in the fire of Hell. And the person who commits suicide using an iron blade, he will have that iron blade in his hand and will perpetually lacerate his stomach in Hell."[1]

To commit suicide, i.e. to deliberately kill yourself, is forbidden (*haram*) in Islam and is a major sin (*kabirah*). There is even a scholarly difference of opinion regarding performing the funeral prayer (*janazah*) of the one who committed suicide. According to Imam Ahmad ibn Hanbal, an Imam should not lead the funeral prayer of an individual who committed suicide (so as to discourage this unlawful act), instead a common or layman Muslim should lead the funeral prayer, for the Prophet Muhammad ﷺ did not perform the funeral prayer of a person who had committed

---

[1] Al-Bukhari, *Sahih al-Bukhari*, book of *al-tibb*, chapter 56, hadith 5778.

25

suicide.¹ However, he did not prohibit the noble Companions from performing the funeral prayer.

Killing someone else (murder)

The beloved Prophet Muhammad ﷺ stated:

1. The first matter that a person will be accounted for (on the Day of Judgement from among the rights of Allah) will be the prayer (*salat*), and (from among the rights of people) the first matter that will be decided between the people will be of spilling blood (unlawful killing).²

2. The wiping away of the whole world according to Allah (Most High) is something very trivial when compared to the unlawful spilling of someone's blood.³

3. When morning comes, Iblis (Satan) spreads out his legion (of devils) and says: "The one who misguides a Muslim today, I will bestow a crown upon him." Consequently, a devil goes and then comes (back) and says: "I remained with a Muslim (and continued to misguide him) until he divorced his wife." Iblis says to him: "(That is no great thing) It is possible that he remarries her." Another devil comes and says: "I remained with a Muslim until he disobeyed his parents." Iblis says to him: "(That is also no great thing) It is possible that he again becomes obedient to his parents." ... Another devil comes and says to Iblis: "I remained with a Muslim (and continued to misguide him) until he committed murder (unlawfully killed a person)." Upon this Iblis

---

¹ Al-Tirmidhi, *Sunan al-Tirmidhi*, chapters of *al-jana'iz*, chapter 68, hadith 1068.
² Al-Nasa'i, *Sunan al-Nasa'i*, book of *al-muharabah*, chapter 2, hadith 3996.
³ Al-Mundhiri, *al-Targhib wa'l-Tarhib min al-Hadith al-Sharif*, book of *al-hudud*, vol. 3, p. 293.

(becomes happy and) says: "You have done something outstanding." And then he bestows a crown upon him.[1]

Allah (Most High) says:

مَن قَتَلَ نَفْسًا بِغَيْرِ نَفْسٍ أَوْ فَسَادٍ فِى ٱلْأَرْضِ فَكَأَنَّمَا قَتَلَ ٱلنَّاسَ جَمِيعًا وَمَنْ أَحْيَاهَا فَكَأَنَّمَآ أَحْيَا ٱلنَّاسَ جَمِيعًا

"If anyone killed a person, other than for murder or (a punishment) for corruption on earth, it would be as if he killed all the people. And if anyone saved a life it would be as if he saved the lives of all people."
[*Qur'an* 5:32]

This means that the killing and murder of any person (whether Muslim or non-Muslim) at the hands of any individual or any government without any reason or justification is equal to the killing and murder of all people. For the one who does not honour and respect any life is the enemy and foe of all humanity. However, a person can face a death penalty for murder or for causing corruption through terror according to the Qur'an, but this would be the responsibility of the government and its judicial system to sentence to death only after the requirements of evidence and justice have been fulfilled. No individual has the right to decide on his own accord to kill someone else.

In spite of this, if an individual takes the law of the land into his own hands even in the name of Islam, then he is a terrorist and he has no relation nor connection with Islam. Just as in every religion of the world there exist some people who are extremists and terrorists, similarly there are such people among the Muslims too. However, to label an entire religion as being a promoter of

---

[1] Ibn Hibban, *Sahih Ibn Hibban*, book of *al-tarikh*, p. 1645, hadith 6189.

terrorism on the basis of these few criminals is complete unfairness and sheer injustice. Just as HRH the Prince of Wales, Charles, stated: "Our judgement of Islam has been grossly distorted by taking the extremes to be the norm. That is a serious mistake. It is like judging the quality of life in Britain by the existence of murder and rape, child abuse and drug addiction. The extremes exist, and they must be dealt with. But when used as a basis to judge a society, they lead to distortion and unfairness."[1]

Countering extremism

Extremists are found in all communities, countries and religions. Although their number is always small; nonetheless, if attention is not directed towards them promptly, then they can become fanatics and terrorists creating much fear and anxiety in the whole society. Therefore, it is an obligation upon the peaceful majority that they look into the root causes of extremism and then provide a remedy for it. For nipping evil in the bud in its early stages is easier, but when it has spread, then countering it becomes difficult. Hence there is the proverbial statement of Desiderius Erasmus: "Prevention is better than cure."

Whilst explaining this type of situation with a practical example, once the Prophet Muhammad ﷺ stated: "The example of those who firmly establish the limits of Allah (Most High) and those who transgress them is like those people who drew lots to determine the seating arrangements on a boat. Thus some of them were allotted seats on the upper deck and others were given space on the lower deck. When those who were on the lower deck wanted to drink some water, they had to pass through the people on the upper deck. So they said to one another that if they were to make a hole in the boat from the lower deck, then (they would attain water by ease

---

[1] HRH the Prince of Wales, *Islam and the West*, a lecture given in the Sheldonian Theatre, Oxford, on 27 October 1993, p. 14.

and) they would not disturb the people on the upper deck with their continuous passing through. Now if those on the upper deck allowed these people to fulfil their intention on the lower deck, then (the full boat will be flooded with water and) all would drown and perish. And if those on the upper deck prevented the hands of these people from making a hole in the boat, then all of them on the upper deck and the lower deck will be saved."[1]

This means that if a fragment of a nation and society is embarking upon a wrongful path and begins perpetrating such acts that would become the cause of destruction for the nation and the state, then it becomes the obligation of the responsible people of that society and nation (such as scholars, academics, religious elders, political and cultural leaders) to put a stop to their endeavours, otherwise the entire nation and society would be rendered devastated and destroyed.

'Adi [*ra*] narrates that he heard from the Prophet Muhammad 🌸: "Allah (Most High) does not cause the common people to suffer punishment as a result of the particular people of sin. However, when they witness wrong among themselves and they do not protest against it whilst having the ability to do so, then Allah (Most High) afflicts punishment upon the common people as well as those particular sinful criminals."[2]

Wrongdoers, law breakers and terrorists exist in every age. However, it is the collective responsibility of every nation that it does not conceal them, rather identifies them; and it does not offer protection to criminals, rather brings them to justice. Just as the holy Prophet 🌸 said: "By Allah! If Fatimah the daughter of Muhammad 🌸, i.e. my own daughter, committed theft, I would give her up to the law to receive the deserving punishment for

---

[1] Al-Bukhari, *Sahih al-Bukhari*, book of *al-sharikah*, chapter 6, hadith 2493.
[2] Ahmad, *Musnad Ahmad ibn Hanbal*, vol. 4, p. 192.

theft."[1] When a nation turns a blind eye to criminals, then slowly and gradually the entire nation becomes engulfed in crime and every individual's life becomes filled with torment.

Imam Fakhr al-Din al-Razi writes that those settlements where polytheists live and they do not transgress against one another in social dealings, then those polytheists are not annihilated in this world merely due to their polytheism (*shirk*) and false beliefs. Rather, torment only befalls upon them when they oppress and transgress against people in their social conduct. It is a well-known saying that worldly governments can function even with polytheism, but *zulm* (oppression) destroys governments; it is unsustainable. Punishment only came upon previous nations because they used to oppress and transgress against the creation.[2]

Abu Bakr al-Siddiq [ra] reports that the Prophet Muhammad ﷺ said: "When the people witness an oppressor and do not take hold of his hands to prevent him from oppression, then very soon Allah (Most High) will inflict punishment upon all of those people."[3]

A proverb attributed to Edmund Burke states: "Evil prevails when good people fail to act." Similarly, there is a statement of Albert Einstein: "The world is a dangerous place to live; not because of the people who are evil, but because of the people who don't do anything about it."

---

[1] Al-Bukhari, *Sahih al-Bukhari*, book of *ahadith al-anbiya'*, chapter 54, hadith 3475.
[2] Al-Razi, *al-Tafsir al-Kabir wa Mafatih al-Ghayb*, in the commentary of 11:117.
[3] Al-Tirmidhi, *Sunan al-Tirmidhi*, chapters of *al-fitan*, chapter 8, hadith 2168.

Chapter Three

The *Fitnah* of ISIS

From the previous two chapters, it should become clear to the reader that at the very core of Islam lies moderation in every aspect of theology and practice; and the practical manifestation of this lies in the very nature and character of the Prophet Muhammad ﷺ, who is described in the Qur'an as a 'mercy for all the worlds'. Moreover, terrorism has its roots in extremism, and extremists can be found in various communities. Not only has Islam condemned terrorism, it has also dealt with its roots by forbidding extremism and cautioning against it.

Today various groups are creating utter destruction and chaos in parts of the world through their extremism and terrorism. Those groups who claim Islam to be the religion they follow are guilty of theological corruption by plummeting themselves into extremism afar from Islam's moderation, and then placing the name of Islam over their transgressions. In this concluding chapter, allow me to comment upon the wrongs of these terrorist groups, in particular the so-called Islamic State, or ISIS (Daesh), so that the readers can clearly see the severe evil of this group, and so that they can also appreciate the clarity of Islam's true message in view of the previous two chapters.

On the outset of this discourse, I have declared the Islamic State, or ISIS (Daesh), to be a *fitnah* (strife), hence I find it is essential to define *fitnah* initially so that the readers can sense why I have referred to this group as a *fitnah*, and also to elaborate on how to deal with this present-day phenomenon.

Understanding the word *fitnah*

Fitnah is an Arabic word. Numerous meanings for the word *fitnah* and its derivatives have been expressed in Arabic linguistic sources such as *Lisan al-Arab* of Ibn Manzur, *al-Qamus al-Muhit* and *al-Munjid*. The meanings include:

1.   *al-dalal* (misguidance)
2.   *al-idlal* (misguiding others)
3.   *al-ithm* (sinfulness)
4.   *al-'adhab* (torment)
5.   *al-qatl* (murder)
6.   *awqa'ahu fi'l-fitnah* (placing someone in strife)
7.   *al-fadihah* (disgrace)
8.   *al-ihraq bi'l-nar* (burning in fire)
9.   *iradat al-fujur bi'l-nisa'* (when the word *fitnah* is linked to women, it gives the meaning of intending adultery and fornication with women)
10.   *al-fatin: al-shaytan li annahu yudillu'l-'ibad* (the one who creates *fitnah* is a *shaytan*, devil, for he misguides the people)
11.   *al-fattan: al-shaytan li annahu yaftin al-nas bi khida'ih wa ghururih wa tazyinihi'l-ma'asi* (the one who creates *fitnah* is a *shaytan*, devil, for he places people into *fitnah* through deception, pride and glorification of sins)

The *fitnah* of ISIS

If the people of the so-called Islamic State, or ISIS (Daesh), are examined in view of the above-mentioned meanings of *fitnah*, then it becomes clear that by acting upon all of the meanings of *fitnah*, they are indeed presenting the picture of a Satanic State, and nothing more. In other words:

1. They are misguided themselves, and are following the way of Satan by misguiding others too.

2. By murdering the innocent people (Muslim and non-Muslim) and by burning them through explosives and fire, they are preparing the torment of fire and disgrace for themselves in the hereafter. In this global village, they are pushing the Muslim community into the fire of mental torment and disgrace too.

3. By glorifying evil and sinfulness, they are deceiving the people like Satan, and by taking free and innocent women as slaves, they are guilty of committing major sins.

How big a sin is *fitnah*?

From the statement of Allah (Most High) in the Qur'an, it is understood that whosoever kills another human being (Muslim or non-Muslim), he has killed all of humanity. [*Qur'an* 5:32] In other words, the unlawful killing of one human being is such a sin that it is equal to the killing of all human beings. Here, I call on all humanity to reflect on the wisdom and greatness of the Qur'an. It is correct that the killing of one innocent soul is equal to the sin of killing all people, but the Qur'an goes further than this and announces:

$$\text{وَٱلْفِتْنَةُ أَكْبَرُ مِنَ ٱلْقَتْلِ}$$

"And fitnah is an even greater sin than killing." [Qur'an 2:217]

This is because *fitnah* becomes the cause of murder and killing. If *fitnah* can be controlled at the earliest, then murder and killing can be prevented. For this reason, Allah (Most High) says:

$$\text{وَٱتَّقُواْ فِتْنَةً لَّا تُصِيبَنَّ ٱلَّذِينَ ظَلَمُواْ مِنكُمْ خَآصَّةً}$$

"And be fearful of fitnah, (because) it will not afflict solely those who do wrong from among you." [Qur'an 8:25]

In other words, if peaceful people do not stop *fitnah* whilst having the ability to do so, then they are indirectly lending support to this *fitnah* allowing it to continue. This is because *fitnah* and corruption occur as a result of what people themselves have done. Just as Allah (Most High) says:

$$\text{ظَهَرَ ٱلْفَسَادُ فِى ٱلْبَرِّ وَٱلْبَحْرِ بِمَا كَسَبَتْ أَيْدِى ٱلنَّاسِ}$$

"Corruption has appeared in the land and the sea because of what the acts of people have brought about." [Qur'an 30:41]

Therefore, it is the individual and the collective responsibility of each nation of the world that when signs of *fitnah* are noticed within a person, they stop that person; and if he does not rectify himself, then they report to the relevant authority. For details on this, refer back to the section on countering extremism. Pondering over the previously mentioned verses, it becomes quite clear that extremism and terrorism, and groups such as ISIS (Daesh), are a *fitnah*, which must be challenged at all fronts. If left unchecked, this cancer will grow and continue to infect, destroying the lives, peace and security of people around the world.

The *fitnah* of extremist groups and terrorist organisations has its own history and over the years numerous groups have emerged with their own agendas, grievances and ambitions – to justify their actions and to give themselves some false credibility to recruit innocent people for their own aims, some of them use the disguise of a deliberate misinterpretation of Islam. In reality, they serve no purpose except creating utter corruption in the world through their actions. Among such groups, the world is witness to the Taliban, Al-Shabaab, Boko Haram, Al-Qaeda, etc. The recent addition to this list of terrorist organisations is what calls itself the 'Islamic State' and is also referred to as ISIS (Islamic State of Iraq and Syria or ash-Sham), ISIL (Islamic State of Iraq and the Levant), and Da'ish (Daesh).

The emergence of ISIS

In 1999, a group by the name of Jama'at al-Tawhid wa'l-Jihad originated which later became known as Al-Qaeda in Iraq (AQI). Over the course of time, this group took numerous names, joined with other groups, expanded their agendas and networks, and eventually became known as ISIS and ISIL, and now merely as the IS (Islamic State).

On 29 June 2014, this group announced the establishment of its so-called Islamic State after taking unlawful control of parts of Iraq and Syria, and Abu Bakr al-Baghdadi was appointed as the *khalifah* (caliph) of this state, i.e. the leader of the believers (*amir al-mu'minin*). Reports suggest the number of his fighters in Iraq and Syria to be between twenty and eighty thousand.

Al-Qaeda and ISIS

In recent times, two organisations have emerged among the terror groups that have become symbolic in the pursuit of their activities, with smaller groups in various parts of the world claiming affiliation to these networks. Initially it was Al-Qaeda and now ISIS (Daesh). It is not my intention to give a thorough comparison between the two as I am not a political commentator. Suffice to say that Al-Qaeda's target appears to be the destruction of the West with attacks taking place in Western countries or their interests abroad. ISIS, on the other hand, seems to focus on revenge against the Muslim rulers and on expanding a state-like structure in these lands. The propaganda of ISIS has been quite sophisticated in attracting young naïve people to travel to this region.

Having said that, it is important to note that Al-Qaeda does not only attack non-Muslims and destroy and ruin their places of worship, but it also considers many Muslims as being non-Muslims too. For this reason, they believe bombing people that are simply performing the prayer in the mosques is also permissible. Similar to Al-Qaeda, ISIS is also an extremist, terrorist group; for according to its viewpoint too, all those Muslims are non-Muslims and deserving of death who do not agree to their ideology. Thus they are continuing to kill and murder those Muslims who disagree with them as well as the non-Muslims in this so-called Islamic State. Some are turned into slaves and others are mercilessly slaughtered and then, by uploading such brutal videos on the internet and social media, they create fear and terror around the whole world.

Both Al-Qaeda and ISIS are following the same path and both have absolutely nothing to do with Islam. Rather, this terrible ordeal is a deplorable and disgraceful conspiracy to dishonour and undermine Islam.

Muslim scholars and leaders from around the world have all declared the so-called Islamic State to be un-Islamic, in particular Dr Ahmad al-Tayyeb, the Imam and Shaykh of Al-Azhar

University, which is the highest seat of Islamic learning in the world with a history of over one thousand years of scholarship. Therefore, no Muslim man or woman should be inviting their own damnation in the hereafter by joining or supporting this group.

ISIS is guilty of heinous crimes against humanity as well as crimes against Islam for which punishment in Hell is awaiting in the hereafter. Under the deceit of creating a so-called Islamic State, ISIS is actually ridding people of their homeland and heritage resulting in deserted and lawless regions where only criminals and those thirsty of blood are welcome.

The caliphate of ISIS

In order to establish an Islamic *khilafah* (caliphate), counsel and consultation is required with all Muslim countries and scholars. Otherwise, civil strife and warfare as well as murder and destruction will erupt among the Muslims, which is something that has been interpreted as misguidance (unbelief and *fitnah*) in the prophetic traditions.

During the farewell pilgrimage, the Prophet Muhammad ﷺ stated: "Soon you will meet your Lord, and He will hold you to account for your actions. Thus do not become misguided after me that you begin to slaughter each other's throats."[1]

'Umar ibn al-Khattab al-Faruq [ra] stated: "A person who pledges allegiance to a man from among the Muslims without due consultation, neither he nor the man to whom he pledged allegiance should be followed. For there is a danger that both of them will end up losing their lives."[2]

---

[1] Muslim, *Sahih Muslim*, book of *al-qasamah*, chapter 9, hadith 4383.
[2] Al-Bukhari, *Sahih al-Bukhari*, book of *al-muharibin*, chapter 17, hadith 6830.

Jihad

Jihad (to struggle and strive) is a sacred obligation that is being misinterpreted and linked to terrorism. The Islamic *jihad* is not terrorism and the actions of ISIS (Daesh) are not the Islamic *jihad* either. The literal meaning of the word *jihad* is 'to do one's best, to exert one's utmost effort to achieve something'.[1] In other words, it is to exhaust all energies of the heart and mind, knowledge and skill, wealth and soul, and hand and tongue; in order to gain something or achieve some objective.

This strive can be in the path of good, just as someone asked the Prophet Muhammad 鷺: "I intend to do *jihad?*" The Prophet Muhammad 鷺 responded: "Are your parents alive?" He replied in the affirmative, so the Prophet Muhammad 鷺 said: "Do *jihad* by serving your parents."[2] This strive can also be in the path of evil, just as Allah (Most High) says:

$$وَوَصَّيْنَا ٱلْإِنسَٰنَ بِوَٰلِدَيْهِ حُسْنًا ۖ وَإِن جَٰهَدَاكَ لِتُشْرِكَ بِى مَا لَيْسَ لَكَ بِهِۦ عِلْمٌ فَلَا تُطِعْهُمَآ$$

"And We have instructed each person to be good to his parents. But, if the parents strive to make you associate with Me that of which you have no knowledge, then do not obey them." [Qur'an 29:8]

In other words, although the parents are worthy of honour and respect, however when they endeavour to incline you towards polytheism or evil, then they should not be obeyed.

For this reason, the Qur'an has added the words *fi sabil Allah* (in

---

[1] Al-Kasani, *Bada'i' al-Sana'i' fi Tartib al-Shara'i'*, vol. 9, p. 379.
[2] Al-Bukhari, *Sahih al-Bukhari*, book of *al-adab* (78), chapter 3, hadith 6038.

the way of Allah) when mentioning the Islamic *jihad* [*Qur'an* 2:218], to ensure that the passion of enmity, evil, lust for territorial control, worldly greed or personal desire do not enter into this *jihad*, and only that *jihad* is intended in which the pleasure of Allah (Most High) is central.

In pursuit of rectifying and bettering the condition, when all peaceful means become unsuccessful, and injustice and oppression becomes unbearable, then in this circumstance armed *jihad* becomes necessary, which is referred to as *qital* (to fight) in Islamic terminology. The value of *qital* in Islam is the same as surgery in medical science, i.e. the patient is only operated upon if all other non-surgical means and medicines have been tested and have failed. *Qital* is also part of *jihad*, but this is its final and last possible form. Moreover, no individual or group can declare *qital*, for the proclamation of *qital* is dependent upon the legal and juristic judgement and reasoning (*ijtihad*) of an Islamic ruler, which would then be binding on the subjects.[1]

The black flags

Nu'aym ibn Hammad, who is the teacher of al-Bukhari, narrates the following tradition:

'Ali ibn Abi Talib [*ra*] said: "When you see the black flags, remain in your lands (and do not help these black flags). Do not move your hands or your feet (i.e. do not help them with your wealth and properties). From there then shall appear a group of weak people (i.e. deficient in religion and moral character), attention should not be given to them, for their hearts will be rigid and hard like pieces of iron. They will claim the (so-called Islamic) state. They will not fulfil any covenant or agreement. They will call towards the truth

---

[1] Al-Zuhayli, *al-Fiqh al-Islami wa Adillatuhu*, vol. 6, p. 419.

(i.e. Islam) but they themselves will not be upon the truth. Their assumed names (aliases) will be parental appellations and they will be attributed to towns (e.g. Abu Bakr al-Baghdadi). Their hair will be soft and free-flowing like women. (This situation will continue) Until they begin to differ among themselves. Then Allah (Most High) will bring forth the truth by means of whoever He wills (and this so-called Islamic State will come to an end)."[1]

To carry a black flag with the declaration of faith in Allah (Most High) and the name of the Prophet Muhammad ﷺ on it, and then to slaughter innocent people beneath it and perpetrate mass killings is an affront and insult to Islam's declaration of faith and the name of its Prophet. These disgraceful acts give weight to the notion that Islam spread by the might of the sword, which is totally incorrect.

Travelling to and joining ISIS

Ma'qil ibn Yasar [ra] reports that the Prophet Muhammad ﷺ said: "The reward of worship during the time of *fitnah* and corruption is equal to migrating to me."[2] In other words, when *fitnah*, corruption and war breaks out, do not aid the terrorists and the murderers; rather, remain at home, occupying yourself in the worship of Allah (Most High) and praying for peace and security. The great reward you will attain for this worship will be like you had migrated from your homeland and settled in the city of Madinah. The excellence of Madinah is such that it removes sins just as a furnace removes the scum from silver;[3] and a person who dies in Madinah will be in peace and security on the Day of Judgement.[4]

There is a point calling for reflection here. A country in which the

---

[1] Nu'aym ibn Hammad, *al-Fitan*, vol. 1, p. 210, hadith 573.
[2] Ahmad, *Musnad Ahmad ibn Hanbal*, vol. 5, p. 27.
[3] Al-Bukhari, *Sahih al-Bukhari*, hadith 4050.
[4] Al-Hindi, *Kanz al-'Ummal fi Sunan al-Aqwal wa'l-Af'al*, hadith 12372.

fire of *fitnah* and corruption erupts, the citizens are being encouraged that if they seek forgiveness from sins and peace in the hereafter, they should remain inside their homes and worship Allah (Most High) and they should not assist the terrorists. On the other hand, the young man or woman from another country, such as America, Great Britain or any European state, who travels to such a place and commits murder of Muslims by joining with the terrorists, that young man or woman should think deeply about what kind of torment he or she is heading towards leaving behind great reward, such as the mercy of Allah (Most High) and the blessings of Madinah? Such a young person is not only ruining his or her own life in this temporary world as well as in the hereafter, but is also creating great difficulties for his or her family and the whole of the Muslim community.

A group of Muslims once came to Imam Ahmad ibn Hanbal and enquired about his opinion regarding overthrowing the ruler of Baghdad. Imam Ahmad ibn Hanbal replied: "Do not shed your own blood and the blood of other Muslims."[1]

Similarly, a group of Muslims came to Hasan al-Basri and enquired about his opinion regarding waging war against al-Hajjaj. Hasan al-Basri replied: "I say not to fight him. For if this is a punishment from Allah (Most High), then you will not be able to remove this punishment with your swords. And if this is a trial (from Allah), then be patient until Allah's judgement comes. He is the best of judges."[2] Concerning Hasan al-Basri, Hammad ibn Zayd states: "By Allah! In relation to (authentic opinion regarding) the spilling of blood and matters of *fitnah*, Hasan al-Basri was from amongst the senior leading scholars."[3]

---

[1] Abu Bakr al-Khallal, *al-Sunnah*, vol. 1, p. 133.
[2] Ibn Sa'd, *Kitab al-Tabaqat al-Kabir*, vol. 9, p. 164.
[3] ibid.

Sunni Muslims and ISIS

Members of ISIS (Daesh) consider themselves to be Sunni Muslims. In reality, however, Sunni Muslims are those who follow the *madhhab* (school of jurisprudence) belonging to any one of the four *mujtahid* Imams – Imam Abu Hanifah, Imam Malik, Imam Shafi'i and Imam Ahmad; they have a connection with the noble Sufis; and they preach Islam with moderation, love and care. On the other hand, these terrorist groups such as ISIS, al-Qaeda and the Taliban have hatred towards the noble Sufis; they demolish their tombs and mausoleums; and they declare those who visit these places as being polytheists and outside the folds of Islam.

Therefore, not merely are the people of ISIS not Sunnis, rather they are not even Muslims; for those Muslims who do not agree to their ideology, they declare them to be unbelievers, deserving of death. If the viewpoints of ISIS are taken into consideration, then this would mean that among the 1.5 billion Muslims around the world, only these eighty thousand or so of ISIS members are actually Muslims, and the rest are non-Muslims. No sane minded individual in the world can accept such a thing. Therefore, O Muslims! Save yourselves from the likes of ISIS, and do not ruin your hereafter through following or supporting the murder of innocent people.

It would appear that this present phenomenon is unprecedented, certainly in today's world it is; however, ISIS can be better described as a group of the Kharijites (*khawarij*) who appeared in the early period of Islam as a religio-political group, pursuing harassment, terror, and brutal murder as well as declaring other Muslims to be unbelievers. This group was responsible for the assassination of the fourth rightly-guided caliph, 'Ali ibn Abi Talib [*ra*]. Remnants of this mind-set have existed over the course of the ages, but scholars have always refuted this ideology, the masses have not accepted it, and the rulers have defeated it.

British Muslims and ISIS

On the 1st of October 2014, the British Prime Minister, David Cameron, declared those British citizens who were travelling out to Syria and Iraq to join ISIS (Daesh) as being 'an enemy of the UK'; therefore, they should be expected to be treated as such. The Prime Minister stated that they have declared their allegiance. Those British citizens who try and travel to Syria or Iraq, everything at the country's disposal will be used to stop them; taking away passports, prosecuting, convicting and imprisoning. Any who have already gone, they may be prevented from coming back.

Whilst supporting this statement of the British Prime Minister, I will add that those who are going abroad to join ISIS, they are not only an enemy of the UK, but they are also an enemy of Islam. All Muslims of Great Britain should be severely condemning such pursuits. If the son, daughter or friend of any person is planning or intending to go and join ISIS, they need to be stopped; and if they do not correct their way, the relevant police authority needs to be informed. In this lies the benefit of the parents as well as the son or daughter. For example, when the police will be informed, the police will make clear that if he or she goes abroad to ISIS, then his or her passport will be taken away and he or she will face prosecution. It is possible that he or she abandons such an intention upon receiving such a caution and warning from the police. In this way, the parents and the son or daughter can continue to live their lives in peace in this country. If, however, the parents do not inform the police and their son or daughter ends up in ISIS, then if the child even returns alive, he or she will be faced with prosecution and possible imprisonment upon return, which will become a worry and burden for all of them.

Therefore, it is an obligation upon the parents to stop their children from illegal and unlawful pursuits to the best of their ability. If they do not stop, then the relevant police authority is to be informed. This is because it is our responsibility as British citizens that we inform the police of the illegal activities of our children, and this is also the commandment and teaching of Islam; just as the Prophet Muhammad ﷺ said: "By Allah! If Fatimah the daughter of Muhammad ﷺ, i.e. my own daughter, committed theft, I would give her up to the law to receive the deserving punishment for theft."[1] Ponder for a moment: Is our son or our daughter more sacred than the daughter of Allah's Messenger ﷺ?

Concluding remark

This so-called Islamic State is in actual fact a group of a few thousand extremist and terrorist people who are dishonouring and defaming Islam by misguiding the impressionable youth. 1.6 billion common Muslims and hundreds of thousands of scholars have declared this so-called Islamic State to be a satanic conspiracy. There is urgent need for responsible authorities and governments as well as media outlets around the world not to refer to these people as 'Islamic State' and not to link their actions to Islam; for this is incorrect, misleading and it does not help the present situation faced by the world. It would be more appropriate to use the term 'Daesh', which is increasingly in use, and the evils of these people can be described with a term attributed to them alone as 'Daeshism' (*da'ish-gardi, da'ishiyyah*).

Recently, the news is also emerging that the foreign youth, boys and girls, who having been lured by the false propaganda on social media travelled to Syria or Iraq, they are now too facing tremendous regret. If they now try to escape from there, they

---

[1] Al-Bukhari, *Sahih al-Bukhari*, book of *ahadith al-anbiya'*, chapter 54, hadith 3475.

themselves face the danger of being killed. Despite these realities, if any foreign youngster, boy or girl, intends to travel to this so-called Islamic State, he or she should ponder deeply over the following one verse of the Qur'an and the following one prophetic tradition (*hadith*); it is possible that guidance is achieved. It is understood from the verse that those people who place believing men and believing women in the state of *fitnah* and cause them harm, they will be made to burn in the fire of Hell on the Day of Judgement. And the prophetic tradition makes clear that those people who take part in the murder of any Muslim not by their hand, but by their mere tongue, they will be deprived of the mercy of Allah (Most High) on the Day of Judgement.

Allah (Most High) says:

$$\text{إِنَّ ٱلَّذِينَ فَتَنُواْ ٱلْمُؤْمِنِينَ وَٱلْمُؤْمِنَـٰتِ ثُمَّ لَمْ يَتُوبُواْ}$$
$$\text{فَلَهُمْ عَذَابُ جَهَنَّمَ وَلَهُمْ عَذَابُ ٱلْحَرِيقِ ۝}$$

"Verily the people who placed the believing men and the believing women in fitnah (caused them harm) and then did not even repent, for them is the torment of Hell, and for them is the torment of burning."
[*Qur'an* 85:10]

The Messenger of Allah (Most High), the Prophet Muhammad stated: "The person who aided someone in the murder of a believer by means of even a few words, he will meet Allah (Most High) in such a state whereby it will be written between his eyes (on his forehead) that this person is in despair of Allah's mercy."[1]

---

[1] Ibn Majah, *Sunan Ibn Majah*, chapters of *al-diyat*, chapter 1, hadith 2620.

Bibliography

Qur'an: the glorious revelation of Allah (Most High) revealed to the final Messenger, the holy Prophet Muhammad ﷺ.

Bada'i' al-Sana'i' fi Tartib al-Shara'i', 'Ala' al-Din Abu Bakr ibn Mas'ud al-Kasani al-Hanafi (d. 587 AH), Beirut: Dar al-Kutub al-'Ilmiyyah, 2003.

Fath al-Bari Sharh Sahih al-Bukhari, al-Hafiz Ahmad ibn 'Ali ibn Hajar al-'Asqalani (d. 852 AH), Beirut: Dar al-Fikr.

Al-Fiqh al-Islami wa Adillatuhu, Dr Wahbah al-Zuhayli, Damascus: Dar al-Fikr, 1989.

Al-Fitan, Abu 'Abd Allah Nu'aym ibn Hammad (d. 228 AH), Cairo: Maktabat al-Tawhid (via shamela.ws – *al-Maktabah al-Shamilah*).

Islam and the West, HRH The Prince of Wales, Oxford: Oxford Centre for Islamic Studies, 1993.

Jami' al-Usul, Mubarak ibn Muhammad ibn al-Athir al-Jazari (d. 606 AH), Beirut: Dar al-Fikr, 1983.

Al-Jami' al-Saghir, 'Abd al-Rahman Jalal al-Din al-Suyuti (d. 911 AH), Beirut: Dar al-Kutub al-'Ilmiyyah, 2006.

Al-Jami' li Ahkam al-Qur'an, Abu 'Abd Allah Muhammad ibn Ahmad al-Ansari al-Qurtubi (d. 671 AH), Dar al-Kitab al-'Arabi.

Kanz al-'Ummal fi Sunan al-Aqwal wa'l-Af'al, 'Ala' al-Din 'Ali ibn Hisam al-Din al-Hindi (d. 975 AH), Beirut: Mu'assasat al-Risalah, 1985.

Kitab al-Tabaqat al-Kabir, Muhammad ibn Sa'd ibn Mani' al-Zuhri (d. 230 AH), Cairo: Maktabat al-Khaniji, 2001.

Mishkat al-Masabih, Muhammad ibn 'Abd Allah al-Khatib al-Tabrizi (d. 741 AH), Beirut: Dar al-Fikr, 1991.

Musnad Ahmad ibn Hanbal, Imam Ahmad ibn Hanbal (d. 241 AH), Istanbul: Dar al-Da'wah, 1982.

Al-Mustadrak 'ala'l-Sahihayn, al-Hafiz Abu 'Abd Allah Muhammad ibn 'Abd Allah al-Hakim al-Naysaburi (d. 405 AH), Beirut: Dar al-Kutub al-'Ilmiyyah, 1990.

Ruh al-Ma'ani fi Tafsir al-Qur'an al-'Azim wa'l-Sab' al-Mathani, Abu'l-Fadl Shihab al-Din al-Sayyid Mahmud al-Alusi al-Baghdadi (d. 1270 AH), Beirut: Dar al-Fikr, 1978.

Sahih al-Bukhari, Abu 'Abd Allah Muhammad ibn Isma'il al-Bukhari (d. 256 AH), Istanbul: Dar al-Da'wah, 1981.

Sahih Ibn Habban, al-Hafiz Abu Hatam Muhammad ibn Habban al-Tamimi al-Busti (d. 354 AH), Beirut: Dar al-Fikr, 1996.

Sahih Muslim, Muslim ibn al-Hajjaj al-Naysaburi (d. 261 AH), Istanbul: Dar al-Da'wah, 1981.

Sharh Sahih Muslim, Muhy al-Din Yahya ibn Sharaf al-Nawawi (d. 676 AH), Cairo: Dar al-Rayan, 1987.

Shu'ab al-Iman, Abu Bakr Ahmad ibn al-Husayn ibn 'Ali al-Bayhaqi (d. 458 AH), Beirut: Dar al-Kutub al-'Ilmiyyah, 1990.

Sirat Diya' al-Nabi, Pir Muhammad Karam Shah al-Azhari (d. 1418 AH), Lahore: Zia-ul-Qur'an Publications.

Sunan Abi Dawud, Sulayman ibn al-Ash'ath Abu Dawud al-Sijistani (d. 275 AH), Istanbul: Dar al-Da'wah, 1981.

Sunan al-Darimi, Abu Muhammad 'Abd Allah ibn 'Abd al-Rahman al-Darimi (d. 255 AH), Beirut: Dar al-Kutub al-'Ilmiyyah.

Sunan Ibn Majah, Muhammad ibn Yazid Abu 'Abd Allah ibn Majah al-Qazwini (d. 273 AH), Istanbul: Dar al-Da'wah, 1981.

Sunan al-Nasa'i, Abu 'Abd al-Rahman Ahmad ibn Shu'ayb al-Khurasani al-Nasa'i (d. 303 AH), Istanbul: Dar al-Da'wah, 1981.

Sunan al-Tirmidhi, Abu 'Isa Muhammad ibn 'Isa ibn Sawrah al-Tirmidhi (d. 279 AH), Istanbul: Dar al-Da'wah, 1981.

Al-Sunnah, Abu Bakr Ahmad ibn Muhammad ibn Harun al-Khallal (d. 311 AH), Riyadh: Dar al-Rayah, 1989.

Tafsir al-Durr al-Manthur fi'l-Tafsir al-Ma'thur, 'Abd al-Rahman Jalal al-Din al-Suyuti (d. 911 AH), Beirut: Dar al-Fikr, 1993.

Al-Tafsir al-Kabir wa Mafatih al-Ghayb, Muhammad al-Razi Fakhr al-Din (d. 604 AH), Beirut: Dar al-Fikr, 1985.

Tafsir Khaza'in al-'Irfan, Sadr al-Afadil Maulana Na'im al-Din Muradabadi (d. 1367 AH), Delhi: Hafeez Book Depo.

Tafsir Nur al-'Irfan, Mufti Ahmad Yar Khan Na'imi, Gujrat: Maktabah Islamiyyah.

Al-Targhib wa'l-Tarhib min al-Hadith al-Sharif, Zakki al-Din 'Abd al-'Azim ibn 'Abd al-Qawi al-Mundhiri (d. 656 AH), Beirut: Dar Ihya' al-Turath al-'Arabi, 1968.

Visit www.alkarampublications.com for more titles by the author including:

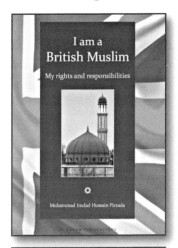

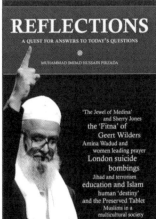

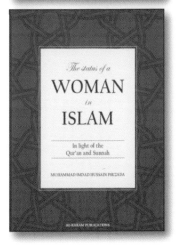